Financial Swagger

The Essentials of Being Financially Savvy

*The Quintessential Financial Book for Students in
High School, College, and Beyond*

**Find more information online at:
www.FinancialSwagger.com**

authorHOUSE®

AuthorHouse™
1663 Liberty Drive
Bloomington, IN 47403
www.authorhouse.com
Phone: 1-800-839-8640

First published by AuthorHouse   06/29/2011

ISBN: 978-1-4567-5982-7 (e)
ISBN: 978-1-4567-5983-4 (hc)
ISBN: 978-1-4567-5984-1 (sc)

Library of Congress Control Number: 2011907101

Printed in the United States of America

Any people depicted in stock imagery provided by Thinkstock are models,
and such images are being used for illustrative purposes only.
Certain stock imagery © Thinkstock.

This book is printed on acid-free paper.

About the Author

Gabe Albarian, a 28 year-old, savvy businessman, shares everything he has learned and experienced throughout his life about personal finance in his first book, *Financial Swagger.*

He has worked in real estate sales, finance, and investment for nearly 10 years and has done extensive consulting work in personal finance for both individuals and groups. His mother and father worked in the real estate finance industry and taught him about the importance of financial responsibility from a young age. Through his financial experience, both personally and professionally, Gabe is able to quickly assess personal finance situations and create feasible solutions and investment opportunities to help individuals thrive.

He earned his undergraduate degree in Political Science at the University of California, Los Angeles and is currently pursuing his Masters in Business Administration (MBA) with an emphasis in Finance at the Marshall School of Business at the University of Southern California. Outside of his business interests, Gabe enjoys volunteering for Children's Hospital Los Angeles and the Mattel Children's Hospital UCLA, playing tennis, skiing, and traveling the world.

To Mom, Dad,
Vicki, and Tamar

Thank you for teaching me *The Essentials* and
providing me with the support to share them with the world.

CONTENTS

INTRODUCTION

Why Financial Swagger?

Financial hardships can create a huge amount of stress and can drive a person to life's darkest moments as they attempt to reverse the financial mistakes they have made in the past.

When you are able to secure your financial life, you will find yourself standing taller and feeling more confident. You will become more assertive in your ability to do and buy things at will knowing very well what needs to be done to maintain a healthy financial lifestyle.

Most of all, you will walk with a lot more swagger…

Chapter One

'Land of the Free' .... Banking

Quick Facts:

- Make sure your bank is FDIC Insured (Federal Deposit Insurance Corporation)

- Always ask about fees and charges for any type of bank account (do not allow fees to be charged to your account – with the exception of a select few)

- Maintain active records of all your transactions to be certain you have the funds available to support the amount you spend

Banking is the gateway to financial savviness, so making smart decisions from the start will help you on your way to a lifetime of financial success.

Before you step foot into any financial institution, be aware that you are giving the bank YOUR money and YOUR business. ALWAYS question fees and charges; remember, no question is a dumb question, especially when you're dealing with your money. Be proactive, listen, and question everything the banker is explaining to you because you may regret it in the future when the bank charges your account a fee you've never heard about. (Don't worry, we'll go over the common fees and charges to look out for later in this chapter.) Furthermore, the bank uses all of the money deposited from its customers and makes their own investments, which makes them a lot of money. Essentially, make the bank work for you, not the other way around, because they depend on your money for their own investments and financial well being.

Make sure your bank is FDIC Insured

First things first, make sure your bank is FDIC Insured. If not, immediately find another bank that is. FDIC stands for Federal Deposit Insurance Corporation and as its name implies, it is a federal organization that insures your individual bank account balances up to $250,000. Now even though you may only have a few hundred dollars or more in the bank, making sure your banking institution is FDIC Insured is still very important. Let's say you only had seventy five dollars in the bank – if your bank isn't FDIC Insured, you can kiss those seventy five dollars goodbye should your bank unexpectedly close its doors or fall into bankruptcy.

There will be signs clearly posted in the bank stating that a certain institution is FDIC Insured. However, just to be sure, also ask the banker inside the institution. During the latest financial crisis, many people who banked at an institution that was not FDIC Insured lost all of their money – don't make the same mistake.

 Get your $WAG on! *Designating multiple people who will receive your funds when you pass away (or POD - Payable On Death) to your account increases your insured amount by the FDIC based on the number of people that are listed as beneficiaries (up to 5 people). For example, if you name your two parents as POD on your account, then your insured amount is increased to $500,000 ($250,000 times 2 – your 2 parents). Source: www.FDIC.gov*

Opening a Checking Account

A checking account is used to deposit all your cash and checks and pay for day to day transactions using a check book, debit card, online banking, and/or an ATM (Automated Teller Machine).

When opening an account, the banker may briefly touch upon the banking fees that may be charged to your account. However, there are more fees than you will ever imagine. Some of the most ridiculous fees you certainly want to avoid include:

- Monthly service fee (also known as an *account service fee*)

- ATM (Automated Teller Machine) fees

- Teller transaction fees (inside the financial institution)

- Online banking fees

- Telephone banking fees

As of February 8, 2011, many major institutional banks will require a minimum amount of approximately $1,500 to waive the monthly account maintenance fees. Be advised that a monthly charge will be incurred if your balance falls below the minimum balance required by your financial institution.

 Get your $WAG on! *At the end of the chapter you will find a comprehensive list of questions to ask your banker when opening your account for a better understanding of the fees you may be charged.*

My personal philosophy is **TO NOT ACCEPT ANY MONTHLY MAINTAINANCE BANKING FEES**. If the banker tells you that the account you have chosen contains such fees, ask for another account that does not charge any such fees or an account that requires a minimal balance requirement to waive the fees.

If your bank insists on applying a monthly service fee then consider the following options:

1. Most banks offer accounts without a fee if you open a **Student Account**. Be careful though – some of these banks waive the monthly fees ONLY during the nine months when school is in session and thus charge you monthly fees during summer months. Double check your bank's policy on this matter if you decide to open this type of account.

2. Many times banks will offer students free accounts at the same banking institution that their parents do all their personal banking.

3. If your employer offers an electronic **Direct Deposit** of your paycheck into your bank account, your checking account may be free of monthly service fees.

4. If you pay a certain number of bills using online banking, your account may be free of any monthly services fees.

5. If your banker tells you there is no way around the fee, find another bank!

Now, this is not to say that ALL banking fees are unavoidable. Some unavoidable fees at most financial institutions include, but are not limited to:

- Check printing fees (when you order new checks for personal use)
- Overdraft fees (charged when your account balance falls below $0.00)
- Stop payment on a check (when you notify your bank to not cash a stolen or wrongfully written check)
- Bank checks (such as a money order, official check, or cashier's check)
- Wire transfers (guaranteed transfer of funds from your account to another)

When opening up your bank account, always ask if any of these fees and services could be provided free of charge. There is nothing wrong with asking…who knows, they may say YES!

Banking Fees and Terms

Your account becomes **OVERDRAWN** when the balance falls below $0.00. If this occurs, you will incur a fee of around $20-$30 (perhaps higher!) for each transaction that is paid and processed when you carry a negative balance. In addition, the dollar amount of the fees will increase nearly every other time you fall below this threshold in the future.

Let's dive into an example of other avoidable bank fees to better illustrate these terms in action:

Chris writes Elizabeth a check for $100.00 however, Chris only has $75 available in his bank account when Elizabeth cashes the check. ***IF THE CHECK IS DEPOSITED AND PROCESSED by Elizabeth's bank (Not a Bounced Check),*** *Chris' account immediately becomes* ***overdrawn*** *and will be charged a fee for a negative account balance as well as a fee for* ***non-sufficient funds*** *since the full amount of the check was not available in his account.*

On the other hand, ***IF THE CHECK IS RETURNED to Elizabeth (Bounced Check),*** *Chris will be charged a* ***bounced check fee*** *and Elizabeth's bank will return the actual check to her by mail, charge her a* ***returned check fee,*** *and immediately* *deduct the amount of the check from her account until a new check from Chris can be deposited.*

The bank has the authority to either cash or return each check if an account does not have the funds available to pay for the transaction. In most cases, the bank will return the check to the person who deposited it (a bounced check).

Here's a brief explanation of the fees mentioned above:

- **NSF (Non-Sufficient Funds) Fee:** A fee charged to Chris' account since he does not have the funds available to pay a check presented for deposit or to be cashed by Elizabeth. This fee applies to all future transactions so long as Chris' account has a negative balance.

- **Bouncing a Check:** A check that is rejected and returned to Elizabeth by her bank (after she made the deposit) because Chris did not have sufficient funds in his account to pay the full amount of the check. As a result of his negligence, Chris' account will be charged a fee. Avoid this at all costs – it not only wastes some of your precious, hard-earned cash, but can also be quite embarrassing!

- **Returned Check Fee:** Elizabeth is charged a fee from her own bank for depositing a check written from Chris that did not have enough available funds.

Most banks offer **Overdraft Protection**, which protects you from expensive fees incurred by overdrawing your account, by either automatically transferring money from an existing savings account or charging the amount due to a credit card that you authorized to be opened at your bank. Be aware that you may be charged a fee every single time a transfer is necessary to cover the amount due in your checking account. However, the fee charged with overdraft protection (around $7 to $10) is minimal compared to not having overdraft protection in place ($20 to $30).

WARNING! If you maintain a negative balance and do not pay what you owe to the bank, your financial institution will eventually close your account and place you in a program called **Chex Systems**, which is basically a black list compiled for review by ALL banks to alert each other of persistently delinquent clients. Essentially, you will not be able to open up another bank account at an institutional bank for a very long time. Avoid getting your name on this list and pay your debts!

Here's a quick summary of the two categories of fees:

Account Fees (normal fees that should be waived)	Avoidable Fees (fees charged out of negligence)
•Monthly Account Maintenance Fee •Check Printing Fees •ATM Fees •Teller Transaction Fees •Bank Checks (Cashier's Check) •Wire Transfers •Online Banking/Bill Pay Fees •Telephone Banking Fees	•Overdraft Fees •Non-Sufficient Funds Fee •Bouncing a Check •Returned Check Fee •Check Stop Payment Fee

Get your $WAG on! *Monthly Bank Statements are a detailed list of all your account activity processed during the past month (they typically list your beginning balance, any deposits and/or withdrawals made, all checks that have been written, and an ending balance; monthly bank statements are available online or by mail).*

Checking over your monthly statements to confirm every deposit and withdrawal is one of the most essential plans of action you can take to ensure that the bank has not incorrectly charged you for a service or made any errors in processing your transactions. If you do find any errors, immediately call your bank's customer service line to correct any changes and confirm the adjustment on the next month's statement.

__Online Banking__ is a great tool that can be used to keep track of your deposits and recent transactions. In addition, you will be able to utilize such tools as paying your bills online, viewing monthly statements, and so much more!

Depositing Funds and Funds Placed on HOLD

Depositing Funds: Banks will usually record your deposits into your bank account(s) by the end of each business day (cash deposits are usually recorded immediately). However, deposits made on a Saturday will be recorded into your account on Monday evening since Saturday is NOT technically a business day (many banks are open as a courtesy to their customers on this day). So, do not spend money that you have deposited on a

Saturday that day or even the next day – in fact, do not spend it until Tuesday because you will be responsible to pay for overdraft charges if your account balance falls below $0.00.

In order to verify the legitimacy of all deposits, banking institutions maintain the right to place a hold on any amount of funds you deposit for many reasons including, but not limited to:

- Opening a new account
- The check amount you are depositing is considerably higher than your current balance
- The check appears to be suspicious

Banks want to keep a close eye on newly opened accounts, so they place an extended hold on most deposits, if not every deposit, for the first 30 to 45 days.

 **Get your $WAG on!** *Holds can range anywhere from 2 to 15 days. However, your bank can verify the legitimacy of a deposited check within about 2 business days if you just ask a manager. If they allege that they don't offer this service then ask to speak to someone who ranks higher at the branch, like a branch manager.*

ATM and Debit Cards

- **ATM (Automated Teller Machine) Cards** can be used at ATMs to withdraw money, make deposits, and check your account balance
- **Debit Cards** can be used as an ATM card as well as a credit card wherever your card is accepted (Visa or MasterCard)

You will not be charged a fee to use an ATM operated by your bank. However, ATMs at other banks and independently owned ATMs will typically add service charges ranging from $1.00 to $10.00 per transaction. Oftentimes, your own bank will even charge you a convenience fee for using third party ATMs. That's two separate fees that can be avoided by simply using your own bank's ATM. Bottom line – try to avoid using ATMs not operated by your bank!

Debit cards can be used almost everywhere just like a credit card, but unlike credit cards with high spending limits, your spending is limited to the available cash balance in your account. Many people use this card much like a credit card, but keep in mind that once the cash balance in your account falls below $0.00, you are immediately charged overdraft fees. Furthermore, you put yourself in jeopardy of incurring fees on other pending transactions and outstanding checks that have not been processed.

Very BASIC Budgeting

Everything you read about budgeting will tell you the same thing: examine how much you earn versus how much you can realistically spend – make adjustments and stick to the plan. Although I commend anyone who can stick to such a plan, I really do believe that the everyday person will NOT do this unless they are in extreme financial trouble.

For beginner's budgeting, I recommend carrying cash in large bills, such as $50s, to restrict the amount you spend on daily transactions. You'll be less inclined to buy that $4 iced coffee if you have to break a $50 – believe me, it works! Some vendors may not even accept larger bills, preventing you from making these smaller, sometimes unnecessary, purchases. Plus, if you budget yourself to $50 a week, you are able to physically see how much you have spent and the amount that remains for your weekly expenditures by simply looking in your wallet.

However much you spend, it is important to keep an emergency fund of about three to six months worth of expenditures for any unexpected events – fees from school, emergency car maintenance, etc. There are plenty of reasons to save for these occasions so make sure to put some money away so that you will not be stuck in a bad situation with no way out.

Actively Maintaining a Check Register

The most thorough way to know exactly how much money you have in your bank account is to maintain a check register. A check register is essentially a spreadsheet that allows you to list all of your deposits and withdrawals, including those from ATMs and debit card transactions, while keeping a running balance of funds that remain in your account. In addition, you must include any applicable bank fees, such as: monthly account fees, ATM fees, return check fees, etc., so that you will have an accurate available balance amount reflected on your check register.

 **Get your $WAG on!** *The moment you write a check, make sure to realize that the money is no longer available in your account. You will be charged a large fee if funds are not available when the check is cashed.*

Now I know that keeping a check register may seem like a difficult task but it's really quite easy once you get in the habit of doing it. Your bank will provide you with a check register that will look very similar to the one on the next page or you can set up your own using a spreadsheet.

Below is an example of how to write a check and what a check register should look like, respectively:

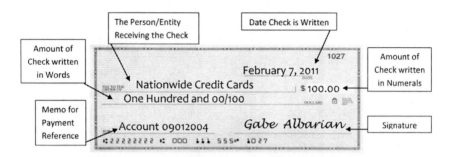

Check Number	Date	Transaction Description	Payment Amount	Deposit Amount	Total Balance
	1/26	Deposit in Bank		$250.00	$250.00
1027	2/7	Nationwide Credit Card Payment	$100.00		$150.00
	2/26	Account Monthly Service Fee	$10.00		$140.00
	3/14	ATM Withdrawal (Not my Bank)	$60.00		$80.00
	3/14	ATM Fee (3rd Party ATM)	$5.00		$75.00
	3/21	Grocery Store Purchases (Debit)	$45.00		$30.00
	3/26	Account Monthly Service Fee	$10.00		$20.00
	4/20	Deposit In Bank		$100.00	$120.00
	4/25	Debit Card – Movie Ticket	$10.00		$110.00

Savings Accounts: Choosing the Right Account

Savings accounts come in different forms, such as a Traditional Savings Account, Money Market Account (MMA), and Certificate of Deposit (CD) Accounts - Traditional and Liquid.

You may find it beneficial to open a savings account if you have a substantial sum of money that you can set aside to earn some interest income. The bank will pay you a pre-determined interest rate based on how much money you have in your account.

Interest rates for all types of savings accounts fluctuate on a daily basis but it is best to shop around for the best rate for the amount of money you intend to deposit. The easiest way to do this is by either contacting the bank directly by phone, visiting a nearby bank branch, or checking bank rates online at www.bankrate.com, which gives you easy online access to research bank interest rates around the nation.

Easy Access to your Money but Low Interest Rates

As opposed to Traditional Savings Accounts, **Money Market Accounts (MMA)** may require a bit more money to open an account.

For this type of account, there may be a limit to the amount of deposits or withdrawals you are able to make – ask your banker about any restrictions. These accounts can be opened with a small balance however, interest rates are tiered according to the amount of money you keep in your account. Again, fees may apply on your savings account if you fall below the minimum balance necessary to keep the account free of charge so be sure to confirm this amount and to not fall below it.

 Get your $WAG on! *If you are in danger of falling below the minimum balance required to avoid fees in your savings account, my best advice would be to close the account and place the remainder of the balance in your checking account so that you will not have to pay any fees. You can always open up another savings account in the future without any penalties.*

Harder Access to your Money but HIGHER Interest Rates

Certificate of Deposit (CD) Accounts come in two different forms, Traditional and Liquid. First, let's take a look at **Traditional CDs**. This account locks your money in for a pre-determined amount of time (ranging from 3 months to several years, on most occasions) during which you are unable to withdraw or add any money until the end of the term. Typically, the longer you lock in your money, the better the rate. If for any reason you need to withdraw your funds from your Traditional CD, you will be monetarily penalized; each penalty amount is different at each financial institution. Ask your banker what the penalty would be if you need to withdraw funds.

Liquid CDs work nearly the same as a traditional savings account but usually offer a higher interest rate. There isn't a penalty for withdrawing funds but, there may be a certain limit to the number of deposits and/or withdrawals you can make per month (please ask your banker).

 Get your $WAG on! *If you are incurring too many fees at institutional banks, try banking at a local credit union where members (account holders) are interconnected though a common bond -- your school, work, or local community. The fees charged for services are minimal. However, your credit union may only have a handful of branches and ATMs available (at most), which may mean that you are charged more fees if you use ATMs that are not operated by your credit union.*

A brief summary of Checking and Savings Accounts:

	Checking Account	Savings Account	MMA	Liquid CD	Traditional CD
Easy Access to Cash?	Yes!	Yes!	Yes!	Yes!	NO!
Interest Income?	NO!	Yes!	Yes!	Yes!	Yes!
Possible Fees?	Yes!	Yes!	Yes!	Yes!	Yes!

Compiled below is a list of questions to ask your banker when opening an account:

- What is the minimum amount necessary to open an account and avoid monthly charges?
- If fees are involved, how much is the monthly service charge?
- Does my account charge a fee for using an ATM or a teller in the bank to perform transactions?
- Is online banking and bill payment included in my account free of charge?
- How much does it cost to order personal checks? Can this be waived?
- Is there a limit on the number of withdrawals and checks I write each month? If so, how many?
- How much will it cost if a transaction is processed and I don't have the funds available in my account? (*Bankers commonly call this "overdrawing" your account; it basically means your balance has dropped below $0.00 – not good.*)
- Does my account come with overdraft protection? (*Overdraft protection prevents the bank from charging you extra fees if you spend more money than you have in your account.*) If so, is it through a savings account or a credit card? How much is the transaction fee for utilizing this service?

Chapter Two

Your Credit (Fico) Score: Who? What? When? Where? Why?

Quick Facts:

- **Credit History Report:** An outline of all your open, closed, and delinquent credit accounts (credit cards, auto loans, student loans, home loans). It includes a history of all of your accounts, how much you currently owe, how many times you have made late payments, and when they occurred.

- **Credit Score** (also referred to as your **FICO Score**): A score ranging from 300 to 850 based upon what is contained in your credit history report. It is generated by an algorithm created by the Fair Isaac Corporation (FICO) that predicts the likelihood a borrower will be 90 days late in the next 24 months on a payment. The higher the score, the less risk you are to creditors, and the better the chance you have to borrow money at a lower interest rate.

The better your credit score, the higher the likelihood of:
- **Lower interest rates on credit cards and loans**
- **Easily renting a house or apartment**
- **Getting the job of your choice**

CREDIT is essential for your future well being!

Your credit is used to finance (or pay) things over time, such as a credit card, student loan, auto loan, home loan, and many other things. Lenders can predict the likelihood that you will pay back your debts on time by inquiring about your credit score (also referred to as your FICO Score).

By monitoring your credit history you will be able to closely detect any problems, such as a late payment or delinquency (severely overdue account balance), and make necessary adjustments to ensure that your credit will improve in the future.

 **Get your $WAG on!** *Credit card interest rates are largely determined by your credit score -- if you have a good score then you will get a lower interest rate. On the other hand, if you have a bad score, you will get a higher interest rate.* **Here's an example:**

> **Ashley** *has a credit score of 725 (a good score) and can easily find a credit card with a 10% interest rate whereas* **Sophie** *has a credit score of 600 and will likely get an interest rate of 25% (or higher) or even have her credit application rejected. If these*

two each carry a balance of $2,500 on their credit card, **Ashley** *would have to pay around $21 per month in finance fees ($2,500 times 10% divided by 12 months) whereas* **Sophie** *would have to pay around $52 per month in finance fees ($2,500 times 25% divided by 12 months) –* ***that's an annual savings of nearly $375 in finance fees! It pays to have good credit!***

Credit Scoring and Why It's so Important

According to the Fair Isaac Corporation, "*When you're applying for credit – whether it's a credit card, a car loan, a personal loan or a mortgage – lenders want to know your credit risk level. To help them understand your credit risk, most lenders will look at your FICO score, which is available from all three major credit reporting agencies*" (www.myfico.com). **Essentially, your credit score is designed to predict the likelihood that a borrower will become 90 days late in the next 24 months.** Don't worry about the three credit reporting agencies right now, stick with me, we'll discuss them later!

Your credit score is based on a scale that ranges from 300 to 850; the higher your credit score, the better. Most people score between 650 and 750 but according to most lenders, a credit score above 720 is a good sign of being financially responsible whereas a score below 600 shows a sign of financial risk. However, there is no need for immediate concern if your score falls below this threshold as I will soon outline ways to boost your credit score.

Easy enough? Well, you just conquered the easy stuff; now comes the nuts and bolts of your credit score and credit history report. Not only do you have a credit score and credit history report from one credit agency, but you have THREE agencies maintaining different credit scores and credit history reports! There are three credit bureaus (Equifax, Experian, and TransUnion) that record your financial data and history in their databases to come up with three different credit scores. Each individual credit reporting bureau calculates your score using similar algorithms, but the information that is reported to each agency may be different and credit scores from all three bureaus may not be exactly the same.

For example, there is a possibility that a credit card or another credit entity may only report to two of the three agencies therefore yielding a difference in the third bureau's credit analysis. However, don't get trapped into thinking that the one credit bureau that may not be aware of your delinquent payments will be your saving grace of your future credit inquires. Usually, your median, or middle, score of the three is viewed as the best indicator of your credit worthiness.

Let's take an in-depth look into how your credit score is comprised, which I have gathered from the Fair Isaac Corporation website (www.myfico.com):

In order to develop a healthy credit history, you must have at least one source of credit that is:

- at least six months old; and

- updated on a monthly basis by a creditor (such as a credit card company)

Your credit score is based solely on what is contained within your credit history report and considers both positive and negative financial information. **There are five parts to your credit score that are based on the following facts and figures.** (Please note that the following information is based on approximate percentages according to the general public's financial activity.)

The Five Parts of Your Credit Score and their Percentages of Importance

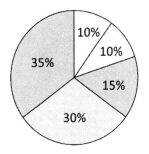

35%: Payment History

30%: Payment Amounts Owed

15%: Length of Credit History

10%: New Credit

10%: Types of Credit In Use

1. **35% based on PAYMENT HISTORY**

Items Considered:

- Have you made your minimum monthly payments on time?
- If not, how recent is your last late payment?

Types of accounts taken into consideration:
- Credit cards, retail cards (from department stores), auto, student, and home loans
- Public record and collection accounts: court judgments and payment delinquencies (severely overdue account balances)

There are three key words when referring to payment history and its effect on your credit score: **recency, frequency, and severity**. For example, the level of severity of a late payment more than 24 months ago is lower than if it were as recent as six months ago.

Levels of severity of a late payment on your credit score:

Last 6 Months	--	HIGH
7 – 23 Months ago	--	MEDIUM
24+ Months ago	--	LOW

According to the Fair Isaac Corporation website, *"Your credit history keeps track of every time you have been late on making payments in increments of 30, 60, 90, and 120+ days; the impact of the late payments increases at each tier"* (www. myfico.com).

Essentially, make AT LEAST the minimum payment on the total balance due ON TIME in order to avoid making a late payment. If not, your account may be sent to a collections agency who will attempt to collect the money owed, charge you a ton of fees, and take action to negatively impact your credit score.

 **Get your $WAG on!** *Court judgments and/or credit items that have been sent to a collections agency, such as a rental housing dispute taken to court or a severely overdue credit card bill, respectively, that have, or have not, been paid in full will remain on your credit history for approximately SEVEN to TEN years (or more).*

2. 30% based on amounts OWED on all your credit accounts

Items Considered:
- The amount you owe on all your accounts
- The number of credit accounts open with unpaid balances
- The amount you have spent versus your spending (credit) limit

The less you owe on your open credit accounts, the better! It's always good to pay down your debts, but remember to spend only what you can pay off at the end of each month. If you have trouble paying the balance due in full at the end of each month, pay a little more than the minimum balance due to decrease the finance fee you will be charged on the remaining balance. Most importantly, don't spread yourself too thin by opening credit accounts everywhere as doing so indicates a high risk of over-spending, which leads to a lower credit score.

Believe it or not, closing a credit card account will hurt

your credit score because it will have an immediate effect on your debt-to-credit ratio (the lower, the better).

For example, if you have three credit cards each with a $5,000 maximum limit ($15,000 total) and total debt between the three cards of $4,500 then your debt-to-credit ratio is 30% ($4,500 divided by $15,000). However, if you choose to consolidate your debt by keeping only one credit card open, your debt-to-credit ratio will now be 90% ($4,500 divided by $5,000), which will result in a guaranteed drop of your credit score. An alternative may be to ask for an increase of your credit limit (the amount you are allowed to spend) from the credit card company(ies) you decide to keep before you decide to close your other credit cards.

3. **15% based on the LENGTH of your credit history**

Items Considered:
- A long, healthy credit history

In this section, it is essential to understand that **the longer your credit history spans, the better – so establish credit early!** The age of all your accounts is taken into consideration and averaged. If you have an account that has been open for 5 years and another that has been open for 1 year, the average age of all your accounts is 3 years (5 years plus 1 year divided by 2 accounts). Essentially, the higher your average account age, the better – do not frivolously open up new accounts as your credit score will suffer.

My general rule of thumb is to NEVER close your first credit card unless there are unavoidable hikes in the interest rate or hidden fees. Having this credit card open and maintaining a healthy history of payments will surely boost your credit score.

4. **10% based on any NEW CREDIT (and INQUIRIES)**

Items Considered:
- The number of new accounts you have opened and how recently they were opened
- How many times you have requested credit (evident through the *credit inquiries* section on your credit history report)

Be cautious when opening one or more new accounts as they may damage your credit score since you are requesting more credit to possibly spend more money.

Each credit inquiry within the last 12 months has a negative effect on your credit score although they remain on your credit history report for 24 months.

 **Get your $WAG on!** *The exception to the rule occurs when you are searching for an auto or home loan within a confined period of time (usually 14 days) since all the inquiries together will only count*

as one inquiry, which is automatically done by the credit bureaus.

5. **10% based on the TYPES OF CREDIT IN USE**

Items Considered:
- A healthy mix of credit accounts as opposed to just one type (credit cards, student loans, auto loans, and home loans)

Open and active credit accounts in the two categories of accounts, known as **revolving** (credit cards) and **installment** (auto, student, and home loans) **accounts**, will raise your credit score.

 **Get your $WAG on!** *Keep in mind that closing an account does not mean that it will be cleared from your credit history report. Rather, there is a section for **Closed Accounts** on your credit history report that is taken into consideration when calculating your credit score. Each closed account remains on your credit history report for around seven to ten years.*

How to Establish Credit

Unfortunately, there are very few ways you can establish your credit score. On the flip side, once you are able to do so, the offers for more credit will start to pour in.

Many times, organizations that require a responsible credit history to open an account, like credit card, auto loan, and cell phone companies, will reject consumer applications if you do not have *any* active credit history. Personally, I had this problem and tried to remedy it by applying for a 'student credit card' meant specifically for first time credit users but my application was denied because I did not have any credit history – quite oxymoronic.

Ways to Establish Credit by use of a Credit Card

1. If your parents are financially responsible and pay their bills on time every month, I suggest that you be added as an **AUTHORIZED USER** (not a co-applicant) on their credit card. Make sure to provide your personal information and social security number to the credit card company so that your credit history report will reflect transactions performed on this account. In about six months after you have initiated this process and maintained a responsible payment history, you will receive your own credit card offers. At this time, submit an application to open your own credit card then call your parent's credit card company and request to remove your name as an AUTHORIZED USER from their account. **<u>CAUTION:</u>** Adding your name as a co-applicant means that you are responsible for the all the money owed on the account for as long as the credit card is active (you will NOT be able to remove your name from the account if there is an unpaid balance or if the other co-applicant

is still using the card); if a payment is late then your credit score will decline. Remember to add yourself as an **AUTHORIZED USER, <u>NOT</u> A CO-APPLICANT.**

2. Apply for a **SECURED CREDIT CARD** at your local bank (if offered) and build credit yourself. When opening a secured credit card, you place a nominal amount of money in a savings account that CANNOT be withdrawn since it is used as recourse to pay back your debts in case you do not pay them yourself. In essence, your spending limit on your secured card is exactly the amount you place in the linked savings account – hence, your debt is SECURED by the money in your account. Just like a normal credit card, you will receive a monthly statement to pay off a portion or all of your debts but meanwhile your payment history will be reported to the credit bureaus. Within months you will receive offers for other UNSECURED credit cards. **<u>BEWARE:</u>** Always ask about any fees that may be associated with opening and maintaining a secured credit card.

According to the CARD (Credit Card Accountability, Responsibility, and Disclosure) Act, credit card applicants under the age of 21 will need to provide evidence that they have enough income to make their monthly payments. This act may not apply to the options presented above because any income documentation necessary in option one is gathered from your parent(s) since you are merely an authorized user; in option two you are insuring your expenses by depositing an amount equal to your spending limit.

Dealing with Credit Problems

Any credit account that is sent to a collections agency, which happens whenever the amount due is severely late, is bad whether or not the balance is paid in full. An account that has been incorrectly entered into collection should be dealt with immediately. After explaining the discrepancy over the phone, ask the credit company who has reported this false information to draft a letter regarding the pending correction and have them forward this letter to the three credit bureaus, which should stop the collection process. Make sure to request a copy of the letter for your own records in case the change is not reflected on your credit history report after 45 days.

Improving your credit score and history takes time. If you are going to buy a big ticket item that requires credit financing, such as a car or house, make sure to check your credit 6-12 months before making the purchase to ensure the accuracy of the information on your credit history report. Act immediately if any corrections or changes need to be made.

According to www.myfico.com, some ways to keep your credit score high include:

- Paying your bills on time
- Keeping low balances on your credit card

- Paying off your debt rather than moving it between credit cards
- Applying for and opening new credit accounts only when you need them
- Checking your credit history report regularly for accuracy (and reporting any errors)
- If you've missed payments, get current and STAY current

Below is an illustration of how your payments, or lack thereof, can affect your credit score:

Action	Change in Credit Score	Current Credit Score
Adam, a college student, opens a credit card and establishes his credit score		700
Adam makes monthly payments to his credit card on time every month for 12 months	+50	750
Adam graduates and doesn't make his student loan payments for three months	-80	670
Adam shops around for a car loan and finally finds one that suits his needs (high interest rate because of bad credit)	-10 (Credit Inquiries) -20 (New Loan)	640
Adam spends the maximum limit on his credit card raising his debt-to-equity ratio exponentially	-40	600
Adam makes monthly payments to his credit cards, student, and auto loans on time every month for twelve months	+80	680

CHAPTER THREE

CREDIT HISTORY REPORT: YOUR FINANCIAL DNA

Quick Facts:

- **Check your credit history report online for free** once a year by visiting: www.annualcreditreport. com. This is the only website that offers credit history reports free of charge.

- **Your credit history report** contains information on all your open and closed credit accounts, how much you owe, when they were opened, if you have late payments, and court judgments filed against you.

- **Identification (ID) Theft** is very common and can happen when personal items and banking information are stolen, either physically or virtually.

Getting a Free Copy of Your Credit History Report

Getting a copy of and understanding your credit history report and how your credit is scored will educate you on how to avoid any credit risks. This will help you establish and raise your credit score, which translates to having better financial options in the future.

Under the Fair and Accurate Credit Transactions Act of 2003 (FACT), you are entitled to a FREE copy of your credit history report from each of the three major credit-reporting agencies (Equifax, Experian, and TransUnion) once a year.

The only way to get a free annual credit history report from each credit agency is by visiting <u>www.annualcreditreport.com</u> and following the appropriate steps online or requesting your credit history report by phone or mail. Any other website offering 'free' credit history reports may come with strings attached, so beware. Unlike these other services, <u>www.annualcreditreport.com</u> provides FREE credit history reports, though they may charge fees for other associated services, such as requesting your credit score. Please note that requests for your credit score and credit history report are completed separately.

Credit history report requests made via the Internet are processed instantly, while requests made via phone or mail will take approximately 15 days to process. Please be aware that the credit bureaus will ask for personal information when processing your credit history report, such as your social security number, date of birth, and other necessary items.

Contact information:

Annual Credit Report Request Service
P.O. Box 105283
Atlanta, GA 30348-5283
(877) FACT – ACT
www.annualcreditreport.com

The three major credit reporting agencies can be contacted directly using the information below:

EQUIFAX
P.O. Box 740241
Atlanta, GA 30374
www.equifax.com
(800) 685-1111
Fraud Alert Line: (888) 766-0008

EXPERIAN
475 Anton Blvd.
Costa Mesa, CA 92626
www.experian.com
(888) 397-3742
Fraud Alert Line: (888) 397-3742

TRANSUNION
2 Baldwin Place, Box 1000
Chester, PA 19022
www.transunion.com
(800) 888-4213
Fraud Alert Line: (800) 680-7289

Since you are entitled to one free credit history report from each of the three credit reporting agencies every year, you can either:

A) Request all three bureau credit history reports at one time; or

B) Request one credit history report every four months from one of the three agencies. **For example**, *if you request a report from Equifax in January, then request your next report from Experian in May, and the third report from TransUnion in September.*

My personal recommendation is to utilize **Option B** as you will be able to detect any changes or discrepancies in your account in a matter of months.

Contents of your Credit History Report

Each credit history report generally includes five categories:

1. Personal Identifying Information – name, address, social security number
2. Credit/FICO Scores (if ordered)
3. Credit History/Information
4. Recent Inquiries for Credit
5. Public Record Information (Court Judgments)

The Credit History section lists current and past credit accounts with loan and credit card issuers. It also states:

- The date a particular account was opened
- High credit limit or original loan amount (spending limit)
- Outstanding account or loan balance (amount you have spent)
- Terms of repayment (number of months remaining to pay debt)
- The number of delinquencies (if any)

Negative history, such as delinquent accounts that have been sent to a collections agency, can remain on your credit history report for seven to ten years and can severely affect your credit score – even if the account has been paid off and closed.

 **Get your $WAG on!** *Refer to the sample credit history report at the end of this chapter for a better understanding of how it may look when you request your own report.*

Ways to Improve your Credit Score

When you request your credit history report and credit score, each credit agency will provide you with a few reasons why your credit score was not higher (commonly referred to as **reason codes**). If your credit score is low, these codes are certainly helpful to getting you on the right path toward improving your credit score.

According to <u>www.myfico.com</u>, common reason codes include, but are not limited to:

- Amount owed on accounts is too high
- High level of delinquency (late payments) on accounts
- Too many credit accounts with money owed
- Too many recent credit inquiries in the last 12 months
- Too many accounts recently opened

Match the codes on your credit report to the percentage breakdown of the credit scoring model discussed in the previous chapter to find out which action would have the greatest impact on your credit score and act accordingly.

Identification (ID) Theft

If your social security number, credit card, bank card, check book, bank statements, or any other item that may contain personal information gets in the hands of the wrong person, your identity and money may be compromised. The theft can be as simple as a stolen wallet or piece of mail or as complicated as personal information found on a computer you have used – the possibilities are really endless.

It is very important to safeguard your personal items and information. Here are some tips to help protect yourself and your personal information:

- Do NOT carry your social security card, passport, or birth certificate with you at all times; rather, keep them locked away in a secure location
- Shred receipts, credit card offers, cancelled checks, and bank documents
- Cancel unused credit cards and cut the card into little pieces
- Do not give out personal information over the phone unless you initiate the phone call yourself
- Memorize (don't write) PIN numbers and passwords
- Make a photo copy of your identification, credit, and bank cards in case of a theft so that you can quickly identify and call the appropriate parties to place an immediate fraud alert or to cancel your accounts

- Do not respond to emails requesting to 'verify' your personal information. You will never be asked to verify your personal information by email. These are sent by imposters claiming to be your bank or any other company
- Sign the back of all your credit and debit cards
- Always remember to sign off when accessing your accounts online (especially at computers in public spaces).

If you feel as though your personal information has been stolen, follow the next steps to prevent any further damage:

- Call your banking institution and/or credit card company and ask them to place a hold on your account to prevent any further fraudulent activity – do this RIGHT AWAY!
- Get a copy of your credit history report and alert the credit bureaus if you find any new accounts that have been added under your name without your authorization. In addition, ask them to place the necessary fraud alerts on all your open accounts.

Sample Credit History Report:

Credit History Report

Personal Information
Name: John Smith
Date of Birth: January 1, 1990
Social Security Number: 123-45-6789
Current Address: 1234 Camberwell Place
                              Los Angeles, CA 90000

Credit (FICO) Score
Equifax: 682

Reason for Credit Score
Recent Delinquencies on Open/Closed Accounts

Credit History/Information
ACTIVE ACCOUNTS

Account Type	Company	Account Number	Balance	Months Open	Delinquencies?
Revolving	Chase	546618064302	$1,260	36	One 30 Day
Installment	Chevy Motor	53582305	$16,549	12	None

CLOSED ACCOUNTS

Revolving	CitiCards	436652064902	$0.00	5	One 30 Day

Recent Credit Inquiries

Date	Company Requesting Credit Record
2/7/2011	Apple Street Bank
4/25/2011	Clothing Store Emporium

Public Record Information

Date	Type	Settlement Amount
9/01/2004	Medical Bill Lien	$350.00

Creditor Contact Information

Chase	(800) 555-1212	123 Chase Drive, New York, NY
Chevy Motor	(800) 555-1213	123 Chevy Drive, Los Angeles, CA
CitiCards	(800) 555-1214	123 CitiCards Drive, Washington D.C

CHAPTER FOUR

CREDIT CARDS:
NOT A FREE SHOPPING SPREE!

Quick Facts:

- **Charge Cards** (offered at department and specialty stores): The balance due must be paid off at the end of each month

- **Credit Cards**: A finance fee is charged to your account if you don't pay the full balance due at the end of each month

- Charge only what you can pay off in full at the end of each month

- Be smart when choosing your first credit card and the rewards you receive – it is best to hold onto this card for a long time to improve your credit score

Credit cards provide for a tremendous amount of convenience when making purchases. At the same time, they can be highly dangerous pieces of plastic that do a tremendous amount of damage if not used properly. Many times, credit card companies give away small gifts, such as school supplies, t-shirts, and many other cheap items, as an incentive for students to open up credit cards. However, there are many lucrative ways to get better benefits from a credit card when making purchases. This chapter will explore the many pitfalls of credit cards but will also direct you toward being savvier in choosing the right credit card for you.

Although many credit cards may have very attractive introductory interest rates starting at close to zero percent for the first few months, be very aware that this low rate will quickly rise to values in the double digits and, in some cases, can soar to approximately 25% (and higher) thereafter! It is important to be cautious of an interest rate that seems too good to be true -- because it probably is! It's always best to investigate before you jump into opening a credit card; you can start by looking up all different options at your local bank, online at www.bankrate.com, or by even calling the institution issuing the credit card with any further questions.

 **Get your $WAG on!** *Credit cards are best used for emergency situations or unique transactions where the cash available in your wallet doesn't cover the transaction value. It may be time to re-evaluate your spending habits if you find yourself using your credit card to purchase your daily meals or small items without paying your balance due in full at the end of each month.*

Fees, Fees, Fees

Finance (Interest) Fees

A credit card always charges a finance fee for any unpaid balance at the end of each month. The amount of the fee is noted in the documents provided by the credit card company as a percentage of the unpaid balance (usually between 7% to 25% - and perhaps higher!). **Let's dive into an example of financing your purchases over a long period of time:**

Suppose you buy multiple items totaling $500 in a given month and decide to pay down the balance by $10 each month until it is entirely paid off. At an interest rate of 15%, the time and charges associated with the transactions are as follows (assuming no other charges are made):

- *Total interest charges: **$289.56***
- *79 monthly payments of $10 totaling **$790.00***
- *Total amount paid: **$1,079.56 (more than double what the items cost)***
- *Total time to pay off $500 balance with charges: **6 years, 8 months***

So much for bargain shopping!

Imagine the time it would take to pay off a debt of thousands of dollars – decades!!! This example is intended to show you that credit card debt not only affects those who spend tens of thousands of dollars but also those who charge a few hundred dollars. I want to encourage you to really think about the consequences of your financial actions, but more importantly, I want you to condition yourself into thinking beyond your immediate desires so that you do not have to deal with the pain and agony of digging yourself out of debt.

So, what do you do if you have multiple credit cards with lingering balances? Well, pay off the one with the highest interest rate or largest balance due first and then move on to the next in sequential order. Try to increase the amount you pay each month to your credit card company to substantially decrease the time it takes to pay the balance in full. In addition, call your credit card companies and ask for a finance (interest) rate reduction if you are a long, loyal customer that pays your bills responsibly every month – be stern and persistent and ask to speak to a manager if you cannot get any aid from the customer service representative.

 **Get your $WAG on!** *Carrying a monthly balance on your credit card while having money in your savings account is counterintuitive because you are being charged more in finance fees each month than you are earning in interest income on the money in your savings account. Instead, either partially or fully pay the balance due on your credit card with the funds in your account to save yourself a ton of money in finance fees.*

Annual Fees

A majority of credit card companies charge consumers an annual fee to use their credit card. These fees can range anywhere from $10 to $150 (and higher!) annually depending on the type of credit card you use. Trust me, if you are earning rewards by using your credit card then you are most likely being charged an annual fee.

Late Fees

Fees for not making your payment on time can range anywhere from $15 to $45 (and higher!) depending on your credit card company. Making a late payment may be reported to the credit bureaus soon after (if you are 30+ days late in making your payment), which will inevitably negatively impact your credit score. If payment is made days after your payment is due, immediately call your credit card company explaining why you were late on your payment as they may consider waiving the late charge if you have a long, healthy payment history with them.

Endless Rewards

Depending on the type of credit card you open, there are many perks that you can receive for making purchases using your credit card. In most cases, not only will you receive a bonus for opening up the account but you will also get continual benefits for each dollar you spend. Charge cards from department stores will offer you a certain discount percentage only on your first day of purchases while well-known banks will usually offer you credit cards with any of the following perks:

- Cash back on purchases
- Points to use on airlines tickets, hotels, and/or car rentals
- Points to use in your bank's point program with a large range of items to choose from including electronics, travel rewards, and more!

Be sure to choose a reward program that works best for your lifestyle as you may be holding on to this credit card for a LONG time – remember, closing credit cards will adversely affect your credit score, not help it. Make sure you make the right decision from the start.

Chapter Five

Financing Life's Biggest Investments

Quick Facts:

- **Student Loans**: Federal loans are a great source for loans but private funding may give you a customized program that suits your needs; www.finaid.org is a great resource for information

- **Auto Loans**: Pre-qualify for a loan to know your budget before you start shopping for a car

- **Home Loans (Mortgages)**: Be smart about the type of loan you choose and be aware of the charges that may come with it

Student Loans

The three most common types of Student Loans are:

1. **Federal Loans**: Commonly known as Stafford or Perkins Loans

2. **Federal Parent Loans**: Commonly known as PLUS Loans
3. **Private Student Loans**: Offered through Sallie Mae or local banks

Two important terms associated with student loans are:

1. **Subsidized**: The government pays your interest payments owed while you are in school. After graduation, you are responsible to make monthly payments to pay off the balance of the loan plus the interest accumulating on the loan.
2. **Unsubsidized**: You are responsible for paying all the interest charged on the loan while you are in school and after graduation. As an option, you can start to pay the amount due on the loan plus the accumulating interest after graduation.

For all things associated with federal loan programs, the best resource is available at your fingertips at **www.FederalStudentAid.ed.gov/funding.** The federal government put this website together to help students get the financial aid they need and deserve to help finance their education.

FAFSA

One of the most important pages on the Federal Student Aid website is the FAFSA, or Free Application for Federal Student Aid, which can be found at: www.fafsa.ed.gov. The only way you will be considered for federal loans is if you and your parent(s) fill out the FAFSA, which is full of all sorts of personal and financial questions to better assess your financial needs. The application becomes available on January 1 for use for the next academic year and has a strict deadline – each state has a different deadline so refer to the FAFSA website to find your state's deadline. Loans are given out according to availability AND level of need so submit your application as soon as possible!

Stafford Loans

In order to qualify for a Stafford loan, students and their families must be able to show financial need. A majority (about two-thirds) of these loans are granted to students whose families earn less than $50,000 per year and the remaining loans are distributed to families who earn less than $100,000 per year.

Repayment of Stafford loans, subsidized or unsubsidized, begins six months after graduation or when the student drops below half-time enrollment. The term of the loan is usually 10 years although extensions may be granted.

Perkins Loans

Perkins loans are awarded to students with exceptional financial needs by the school they are attending and are supplied by a limited amount of federal funds. These loans are subsidized and repayment begins nine months after graduation, or when the student drops below half-time enrollment; the repayment period is 10 years. The limit for undergraduate students receiving a Perkins loan is $5,500 per year with a cumulative limit of $27,500.

PLUS Loan (Parent Loan for Undergraduate Students)

Both students and their parent(s) apply for the PLUS loan that can cover the entire cost of their tuition (minus the amount of any other financial aid received from Stafford or Perkins loans) without any cumulative limit throughout a student's undergraduate years. The responsibility of payment for this unsubsidized loan falls upon the parent(s) and the accumulation of interest on the amount of the loan begins 60 days after the funds from the loan have been deposited into your school tuition account; the repayment period is 10 years. Your parent(s) must have a very good credit score (over 720) in order to qualify for this loan.

Private Student Loans

If you or your family does not qualify for any or all of the federally funded loans then finding a private loan may be your best bet. Either your local bank or an entity named Sallie Mae (www.salliemae.com), which is focused on financial services for education, is your best resource for private loans.

Scholarships

Hundreds of thousands of scholarships totaling millions of dollars are offered and rewarded to students each and every year. This is essentially free money used to cover the cost of their tuition. Scholarship types include (but are not limited to) academic, athletic, artistic, cultural, and philanthropic excellence of which each has a different application and necessary qualifications. The easiest way to search for scholarships is by visiting www.fastweb.com or by asking your college counselor about available scholarships in your community.

In addition, individual states and universities offer their own scholarships – ask your college counselor how to proceed with getting more information about these scholarship opportunities.

The same pool of students eligible for Perkins loans may also be eligible to receive a federal **Pell Grant**. It is an award of up to $5,500 given by the federal government that does NOT have to be re-paid. The application for this grant can be found on the Federal Student Aid website.

A brief summary of Student Loans:

Loan Program	Program Details	Annual Award Limits
Stafford (Subsidized)	•Lender pays interest while you are in school •Payment starts 6 months after graduation or when student falls below half-time status	•1st Year: $5,500 •2nd Year: $6,500 •3rd+ Years: $7,500 •Cumulative limit: $23,000 for dependant students
Stafford (Unsubsidized)	•Student pays interest while you are in school (added to total balance owed) •Payment starts 6 months after graduation or when student falls below half-time status	•1st Year: $5,500 •2nd Year: $6,500 •3rd+ Years: $7,500 •All figures include subsidized + unsubsidized annual loan amount limits
Perkins (Unsubsidized)	•Student pays interest while you are in school (added to total balance owed) •Payment starts 9 months after graduation or when student falls below half-time status	•Undergrads: $5,500 per year with a cumulative limit of $27,500
PLUS Loan (Unsubsidized)	•Parent(s) pay interest while you are in school (added to total balance owed) •Interest charges on accumulated balance begin 60 days after money is dispersed	•Cost of attendance minus any other financial aid received
Private Loans	•Different options offered at Sallie Mae or banks	•Visit your bank or www.salliemae.com for more details

Auto Loans

Buying a car can be a great achievement in your life, but you must know the basics of financing a car and what it involves before even starting to search for your next sweet ride.

The first question will always be, "How much can you afford?" Your monthly car payment (including insurance and registration) should be approximately 10% of your monthly income. In addition, you should attempt to make a cash down payment on the car to keep your monthly payments lower than they would be without one.

The best way to find the right payment that works within your budget is to pre-qualify for a loan at your local bank. During this process, the banker will request your credit history report and credit score from the three credit bureaus, inquire about your employment, yearly income, and gather several other pieces of personal information. It is important to be honest with the questions being asked as you will be able to correctly identify the purchase price that works within your budget.

Interest Rates

Depending on your credit history report and credit score, the interest rate on your car could be as low as 1.0% or as high as 15%. When you pre-qualify for a loan at your bank, make sure to compare rates at neighboring banks in addition to the dealership where you are purchasing your car to find the best interest rate.

I can't say this enough – **YOUR CREDIT IS SO IMPORTANT TO EVERY ASPECT OF FINANCING PUCHASES THROUGHOUT YOUR LIFE!** It dictates the interest rate you will receive on every item you finance. Be responsible and take pride in maintaining a strong credit score!

Leasing versus Purchasing

Plain and simple: I don't recommend leasing a car unless you have tons and tons of money to waste. Lease terms are for a finite amount of time yet the lifetime of cars is far beyond the periods allotted in lease agreements.

When you purchase a car, you finance it to slowly pay off the balance due on the loan. Your best bet is to keep on driving your car after you have paid off the total balance due on your auto loan so that you may enjoy many months and years without having to make a car payment.

Used Cars

Buying a used car can be tricky, but there are tools to ensure that you know the true value and history of a used car before you purchase it.

- Kelly Blue Book (www.kbb.com) is a great resource to accurately price a used car based on its make, model, year built, mileage, and condition.
- A Vehicle History Report from such companies as CARFAX will provide you with a comprehensive review of the ownership, accident, and service histories (and so much more!).

- A Complete Bill of Sale provided by the Department of Motor Vehicles (commonly referred to as a Pink Slip) rightfully transfers ownership when the transaction is complete.

Make sure to look into all the above mentioned items and make an informed decision about your next used car purchase.

Home Loans (Mortgages)

The American dream is to own a home – the white picket fence, a backyard with a pool, or whatever characteristics you may want when purchasing a place of your own. Home ownership is indeed a great milestone in anyone's life. Finding your dream home may be fun, but getting a loan with manageable payments that suit your lifestyle can prove to be a challenge. Home loans are usually made payable over 360 monthly payments (or 30 years).

There are two items that are always taken into consideration when getting a home loan:

- The amount of the down payment (paid in cash before you own the home)
- The amount of the loan financed through a lending institution, such as a bank (the remaining balance of the purchase price of the home minus the down payment)

There are many loan programs that are offered to consumers depending on the amount of their down payment. First time homebuyers may qualify for a government supported **FHA Loan**, which is sponsored by the Federal Housing Administration, with a down-payment as low as 3.5% of the purchase price.

Whenever your loan value is greater than 80% of the market value (meaning your down payment is less than 20%), lenders will add PMI to your payments, or **Private Mortgage Insurance**. Lenders require that the value of the loan be insured because the total amount of money owed to them is very high. By insuring the money they lend you, lenders can recover most or all of the money they would stand to lose if you stopped making your monthly payments. As the borrower, you are required to pay for PMI although the lender is the only party to benefit from it.

The most common type of loan is frequently referred to as an '80-20' loan. This loan requires a down payment equal to 20% of the purchase price with a loan that equals 80% of the purchase price. PMI is not required since the 20% down payment threshold is met.

Get your $WAG on! *There are typically two types of interest rates offered when you apply for a home loan –* **Fixed Rate** *and* **Adjustable Rate**. *Plain and simple, I would advise you to choose a fixed rate loan for more stability and predictability of your monthly payments as they remain the same for the entire duration of your loan. A majority of people who had an adjustable rate loan in recent years were those who fell victim to the financial crisis and, in many cases, lost their home. As the name implies, the interest rate adjusts after a pre-determined number of years and many times, the interest rate is higher and borrowers have a difficult time making their new, higher payments. Trust me, the stability of a fixed rate loan is the best move you can make.*

Getting a Home Loan

Typically, your monthly loan payment (including property taxes and insurance) should not exceed 30% of your monthly income. I suggest pre-qualifying for a home loan at your local bank to better assess your target purchase price before you begin to shop for your new home.

When applying for a loan, your home loan specialist will immediately ask you for the following documents:

- Personal and employment information
- Your social security number to gather your credit history report and credit score
- Two most recent state and federal annual income tax returns

- A copy of your most recent paycheck(s)
- Two most recent monthly bank statements

Fees Involved:
- **Appraisal:** When purchasing a home and applying for a loan, the bank determines the value of the property by ordering a professional appraisal
- **Escrow Company:** A company who acts as the intermediary for the transfer of funds between the bank, the buyer, and the seller
- **Title Company:** A company who guarantees that the property is successfully transferred into your name with ONLY the home loan(s) you applied for when purchasing a home

The appraisal fee is a flat fee determined by each individual lender that normally costs about $300 to $600 depending on the size of the property. Escrow and title fees are based on a flat fee plus a percentage of the purchase price over the flat fee.

The entire process of getting approved for a home loan may be challenging because of the countless requests from your home loan specialist however, you will be rewarded for all your hard work when you receive the keys to your new home.

Chapter Six

You're NEVER too Young to Invest

Quick Facts:

- **Stock Trading**: Be passionate about the company you invest in; stock trading can be a great way to earn money over a long period of time.

- **Mutual Funds and Retirement Accounts:** You are never too young to invest – you can be a millionaire when you retire!

- **Real Estate**: Buy during your college years and rent out rooms to your responsible friends.

If you think that you are too young to start saving for your future then I'm afraid you are wrong. There are so many ways to invest: stock trading, IRAs and/or 401(k), 403(b), purchasing real estate, and so much more – the options are endless – it just takes a little effort and some basic knowledge.

Stock Trading

Stock trading is one of the best ways to make money over a long period of time – the more a company grows, the more you make!

When you own stock in a publicly traded company (those that are actively traded on the New York Stock Exchange or NASDAQ) you theoretically own a very small, fractional portion of the company. Buying a few shares of stock certainly does not make you the Chief Executive Officer, but you do have certain rights as a partial owner, such as, but not limited to: attending annual meetings and occasional voting rights on stockholder issues.

Choosing a publicly traded company on the stock market to invest in may be a difficult decision. One of the primary rules I utilize is to ONLY invest in a company you feel passionate about – their product offerings, their management team, their future prospect -- anything to spark your interest. Furthermore, keeping an eye on company news about such things as quarterly financial reports, product releases, as well as factors that may have a negative impact on a company's valuation, such as legal issues, will make you more knowledgeable about the company. I'm not asking that you know and understand everything about the company, but believing in its future growth is one of the most important factors to take into consideration when making an investment.

Sample stock information for the Fair Isaac Corporation (FICO) from May 25, 2011:

Fair Isaac Corporation **Price: 28.80 ⬆ +0.41/+1.44%**	Symbol (NYSE): FICO
Previous Close: **28.39**	52 Week High: **31.81**
Today's Open: **28.26**	52 Week Low: **20.37**
Day's Range: **28.26 – 28.97**	Dividend Rate (Per Share): **0.08**

*Data from May 25, 2011
(www.CNNmoney.com)

When you begin to research a publicly traded company's stock price on a financial website like www.CNNmoney.com, some items to consider include **the current price of one unit** of stock in the company (as seen under the name of the company), the amount/percent the price has changed since the previous trading day, and the **52-week high and low** of the stock price. Also take the time to view charts on how the stock has performed in the past day, week, month, and year. The **Previous Day Close Price** shows the value of the stock at the end of previous trading day whereas **Today's Open Price** shows the price at the beginning of the current trading day. The price discrepancy in the two values is due to trading that is completed after the market has actively closed and before it opens the next day. The **Day's Range** displays the daily range of the stock price during active trading hours. All of these items are good indicators of a stock's recent valuation and performance. You can further research the news associated with high and low stock values of a specific company to find what enhances or hurts its profitability.

Dividends are monetary earnings that the company distributes to its stockholders when they feel as though they will not be using those funds for investments in the near future. The amount you receive when a dividend is announced is based upon the number of stocks you own. For example, if the announced dividend is $1.00 and you own 10 shares of stock in the company then expect $10.00 to be deposited into your stock trading account. Cha-Ching!

Discount stock trading firms like Fidelity and TD Ameritrade offer online trading at nominal prices. Visit their website or speak to one of their customer service representatives for more information.

Mutual Funds, IRAs – Roth vs. Traditional, 401(k), 403(b)

A mutual fund is a stock and/or government bond investment account that pools money together from thousands of people. The money in each mutual fund is handled by individual fund managers who are responsible for the deposited funds and only invest in organizations according to the type of fund (there are hundreds of funds to choose from that will fulfill your preferences). For example, a fund may only invest in West Coast companies whereas another would only invest in Chinese companies; in addition, many funds are sector specific (real estate, technology, utilities, government bonds, etc).

An IRA, or Individual Retirement Account, 401(k), and

403(b) all utilize mutual funds to maximize the amount of money you earn for retirement by giving you hundreds of funds to choose from that fit your preferences. It is critical to figure out what type of portfolio you wish you have and to invest accordingly:

1. **Aggressive (High Risk)** -- a majority of the fund is invested in stocks
2. **Balanced/Growth (Average Risk)** -- a mix of bonds and stocks
3. **Conservative (Low Risk)** -- a majority of the fund is invested in bonds

An aggressive portfolio would consist of publicly traded companies on the stock market that have the potential for a large return, like 15-20% or higher, whereas a conservative portfolio consists of government and municipal bonds that may yield around 2-3% in returns. Typically, in your younger years it is advisable to take more risks and thereby invest aggressively but as you get older and ultimately near retirement one should verge more towards balance/growth and then conservative funds, respectively.

The best strategy is to invest in a number of different funds that will have the potential to earn high returns while still having safe investments to always yield a constant revenue stream. The term **diversification** is used a lot when referring to retirement accounts so be aware that your account doesn't need to be strictly aggressive or conservative but rather, a healthy mix of all three portfolio types previously mentioned may be a great way to see good financial return while controlling your risk.

Types of Retirement Accounts

The following are the most common retirement accounts and their benefits:

- **Roth IRA**: Offered to anyone who earns a yearly gross income of less than $107,000 (in 2011)

- **Traditional IRA**: Offered to anyone who earns a yearly gross income totaling more than $107,000 (in 2011)

- **401(k):** Offered by most For-Profit Organizations (Fortune 500 & Privately owned companies) to their employees

- **403(b):** Offered by most Not-For-Profit Organizations to their employees

A brief summary of Retirement Accounts:

	ROTH IRA	TRADITIONAL IRA	401(k) or 403(b)
Maximum Contribution	$5,000 for 2011	$5,000 for 2011	$16,500 for 2011
Tax Effect of Contributions	Fully Taxed	Tax Deductible	Pre-Tax Income Invested
Tax Effect on Growth Over Time	Tax Free!	Tax Deferred	Tax Deferred
Tax Effect when Funds are Withdrawn at Retirement	Tax Free!	Fully Taxed	Fully Taxed

 **Get your $WAG on!** *Contributions to your 401(k) or 403(b) are pre-tax money (before Uncle Sam takes his money from your paycheck) and best of all, many companies match your contributions up to a certain limit each year – FREE MONEY! You would be silly not to take advantage of this opportunity!*

Although the money you deposit into your Roth IRA is taxed as earned income each year when you file your annual tax return, the accumulated funds withdrawn at retirement are TAX FREE! (Everything you have earned is yours to keep!) Alternatively, the money you deposit into your Traditional IRA can be subtracted (deducted) from your annual income on your tax return, which means you owe less to the government in taxes each year, though at retirement the accumulated funds are fully taxed as income. (You must pay taxes on the money you withdraw from your retirement account.)

INVEST EARLY!!! It is important to begin depositing funds, regardless of the amount, into a retirement account as early as possible. By doing so, you will earn more interest income on your invested money much faster than someone who begins their large deposits later in life. **Let's look at an example that illustrates this point:**

Grace deposits the annual maximum contribution of $5,000 into her IRA at the beginning of each year from age 20 to 30 ($50,000 total cash contribution) whereas **John** deposits $5,000 into his IRA at the beginning of each year from age 30 to 65 ($175,000 total cash contribution). With a 10% return each year, who do you think will have more money in their IRA at age 65? **Answer: GRACE!**

The actual calculated figures show us that **Grace** *earns* **$2,463,342.71** *whereas* **John** *earns* **$1,490,634.03 – nearly One Million Dollars less!**

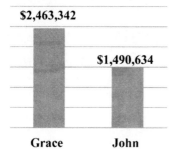

Total Earnings at Age 65

$2,463,342

$1,490,634

Grace   John

·**Grace:** $5,000 deposit per year from age 20 to 30
Total Deposited: $50,000.00

·**John:** $5,000 deposit per year from age 30 to 65
Total Deposited: $175,000.00

This money can be withdrawn penalty free at or after age 59 ½ otherwise a penalty may be assessed. Please ask your investment advisor for more details.

Depending on the brokerage firm, you may only have to deposit a couple hundred dollars to open a retirement account. Schedule an appointment with a financial adviser from a discount investment firm, such as Fidelity or TD Ameritrade, to discuss what type of retirement account best suits your needs.

It is important to monitor your funds often and perhaps make any changes to your retirement account after discussing it with an advisor at the investment firm to constantly increase the amount of money you are earning.

 **Get your $WAG on!** *Institutional banks offer their own type of retirement funds, but may charge substantial service and management fees based on a percentage of the amount in your account. Discount brokerage firms almost always offer their accounts free of charge.*

Purchasing Real Estate

In my opinion, the best way to make a long-term investment is in real estate. Yes, the market has been quite volatile lately (as of 2011) but every economic market is cyclical and the real estate market is not an exception.

My advice would be to look to purchase a piece of property close to school during your years in college and rent out the other rooms to some of your trustworthy friends. This way, you can use the money you collect from your renters to pay for part or all of your mortgage payment, pay close to nothing yourself, and earn **EQUITY** in your property (the difference between the amount an investment is currently worth minus what you originally paid for it) throughout your years in college! Don't waste your money renting an apartment that doesn't have any income potential. Rather, put that money to good use and watch it grow!

As a student, you may have some difficulty qualifying for a home loan, but your parents may qualify for a loan on your behalf. You can responsibly pay the monthly amount due to the bank yourself from the money you collect from your renters. Who knows – you just may make some money for yourself each month after all the bills are paid!

Finding the Right Property
When looking to purchase a condominium, townhouse, or house, it is important to work with a local Real Estate Agent who knows the area and can direct you to the best properties within your budget. In addition, some preliminary questions you should consider when planning to purchase a property include:

- How long will I own this property?
- How close do I want to live to campus?
- What is average rental rate in the area?
- How much will I make my renters pay?
- How many renters do I want to live with?
- Do I include the cost of utilities in their rent?

The advantage of having renters in your property is that you may end up paying less each month than if you lived alone in a rental property. For example, if you purchase a three bedroom home with a monthly loan payment of $1,200, research that the room rental rate in the area is $500, rent two bedrooms to your friends at $500 a piece ($1,000 total), then you will pay only $200 in rent (not including any utilities)!

In terms of where to look for a property, staying close to campus is ideal since there is a constant flow of new and returning students (renters!) each year. Naturally, the prices of these properties will be higher than others but you may find other properties within a short distance from campus that may be considerably less in price and offer you a bigger living space.

Finally, remember that this property is not a fraternity or sorority house but rather an investment property. You will be responsible to fix and pay for any damage done to the property so, make sure to think wisely when picking renters and hosting social gatherings.

Chapter Seven

Getting the Job – Done!

Quick Facts:

- Apply to jobs that are relevant to your educational and/or professional experience.

- During an interview: be prepared, be professional, and be proactive!

- Prepare a professional resume (and always carry around multiple copies).

- Your credit history report may be checked when applying for a job.

Things to Remember when Applying for a Job

Getting a job has become increasingly difficult because companies are looking to tighten up their budgets by re-evaluating the number of employees needed to get the job done. It is very important that you make sure to apply for jobs that are relevant to your educational and/or professional experience and not to arbitrarily apply for every available job. Hiring managers and human resources representatives receive hundreds, if not thousands, of resumes for one single job opening. As a result, they resort to using advance word search programs to sort through every resume, which searches for specific keywords relevant to the job and selects only a handful of resumes for review.

Once you get the call for a job interview, you should treat every single one the same – be prepared, be professional, and be proactive. Let's dive right into it. Below are eight very important points to consider throughout the job interview process:

Before the Interview
1. **Mentally prepare yourself with questions that the interviewer may ask you according to the job description.** You can be certain the hiring manager will ask about your experience and how it applies to the job but also what you will be able to offer to the organization, both personally and professionally. In addition, looking into the intricacies of the job description may give you a better understanding of what the job requires and allow you to predict the interviewer's questions and prepare accordingly.

2. **Print out multiple copies of your resume when you go to an interview.** You may meet with one person or you may meet with five people – you never know but you always want to be prepared. Many times, hiring managers will want their team

to interview you as well so that they can assess how you will fit into the work environment. Keep your resumes in a nice folder to show professionalism.

3. **Dress for Success!** I don't care if you are preparing for a job interview for a janitorial position or for the Chief of Staff for the President of the United States – always look professional and presentable. Don't forget to have your clothes cleaned and pressed to look your best! You can only make ONE first impression.

During the Interview

4. **Your interview starts the moment you check-in**. Leave your cell phone in the car, sit up straight, and quietly review your resume one last time to make sure you touch upon all the points you want to talk about. Most of all, be respectful to everyone you encounter throughout the process as they may be giving input to the hiring manager or human resources representative about your character.

5. **The initial greeting**. A firm handshake is always a sign of confidence; make sure to substantiate it by making eye contact while formally introducing yourself: "Hello, my name is _____ . It is very nice to meet you. Here is a copy of my resume." Have a seat and mind your posture – sit up straight with your hands placed nicely in your lap. Don't fidget or play with your folder.

6. **Keep it professional but show that you are engaged in the conversation**. Nodding your head and adding relevant comments or questions at appropriate times will show an increased level of interest in the job. Most of all, be a good listener as it shows that you will take direction well when on the job.

7. **Compensation – don't discuss it at the interview! (Unless you are asked.)** Most of the time, compensation will be outlined in the job description, but when it isn't, complete the interview first then discuss it with either the human resources representative or the hiring manager at a later time. At this time, other benefits, such as medical benefits and retirement funds, can be discussed at length.

After the Interview

8. **ALWAYS, ALWAYS, ALWAYS send a thank you email one day after the interview followed up with a HANDWRITTEN thank you note to everyone who interviewed you.** Thank them for their time, explain what you learned, what you felt about the working environment, and how excited you are to be considered for the position. I believe this is one of the most important aspects of the interview process as it shows responsibility and general interest in the position.

Interviews: The three most commonly asked questions:

1. **Tell me about yourself?** Some candidates answer by saying, "What do you want to know?" WRONG!!!!! Hiring managers look at your resume but only you are able to breathe life into it. When you are asked this question, reply with your age, what High School/College you attend/graduated from, your professional interests and experience, why you are interested in the current position, and what makes you a good candidate for the position. Practice, be brief, and try to keep it to around 20 to 30 seconds but use your time effectively.

2. **Why are you interested in working for our company?** Your answer should be based on background information you have found on the company website and other relevant publications – search into their past, what type of projects they are working on, and how you can add to the future profitability and development of the organization.

3. **Where do you see yourself in 10 years? 15 years? 20 years?** Be realistic when answering this question. Obviously, it is never right to say, "I want to take all the clients and experience I have learned from this company and create one of my own." Show the hiring manager that you are committed to the organization and its continued development – whether you choose to stay with the job for years to come, or not. By asking this question, hiring managers want to hear about your own aspirations and drive to succeed.

Items to Consider when Searching for a Job

Credit & Criminal History checked: If you didn't believe that credit was important in the previous chapters, it reappears once again! In the eyes of employers, responsible spending habits and good credit are indicators of a reliable employee. Make sure to finalize any corrections to your credit history report before applying for a job. In addition, your criminal history is examined to make sure you truthfully disclose everything you included in your job application.

Social Media: A good thing or not? In my opinion, I find that deactivating your social media accounts during the job search process may be to your advantage. Hiring agents always want to know more about their potential employees and they may find some photos or comments on the Internet that may not work to your benefit. Instead, subscribing to professional networking sites like LinkedIn (www.linkedin. com) can effectively showcase your professional experience.

Business Cards and a Website: Having business cards with your personal contact information for distribution is always a great idea – you never know who you'll meet when you are out and about! What I love even more is having your own personal website with your photograph, biographical information, resume (link a printable version, too!), and your contact information. There is no better way to have people find your information than on your own personal website with everything they need to know and consider available at their fingertips!

An Example of a Professionally Formatted Resume:

John Smith
1234 Camberwell Place, Los Angeles, CA 90000 · (123) 456-7890 · John.Smith@FinancialSwagger.com

EDUCATION

University of Southern California, Marshall School of Business   Los Angeles, CA
Master of Business Administration   May 2012

University of California, Los Angeles   Los Angeles, CA
Bachelor of Arts, Political Science   June 2005

Chaminade College Preparatory   Los Angeles, CA
          June 2001

EXPERIENCE

Metropolis Realty Group   Los Angeles, CA
President: Sales, Finance, and Investments   present
Real Estate firm that specializes in sales to our clients as well as expanding internal investment opportunities
- Real Estate Sales to clients with a price range of $100,000 to $15,000,000 for Single Family Residences
- Real Estate Sales of Multi-Family and Commercial Properties
- Negotiate directly with major bank and lender representatives on short-sale and bank-owned transactions based on future value of assets
- Manage and maintain rental properties in the company's expanding portfolio
- Create financial models to evaluate project profitability scenarios

The Television Entertainment Company –International Television   Los Angeles, CA
Financial Analyst   2008-2009
Assist in the account research and strategy development for key global partnerships
- Perform monthly account reconciliation, overhead allocations, P&L statements, and journal entries
- Assist in creation of quarterly financial statements and research into cost centers
- Support global units and research future opportunities in other global markets

Superior Banking Group   Los Angeles, CA
Business and Premiere Banking Teller   2007 - 2008
Provide banking solutions to business and high balance customers
- Handle day to day banking needs of clients
- Award winning salesperson of accounts, mortgages, investments, and financial services

One Final Note . . .

Knowledge is power and I sincerely hope that by reading **Financial Swagger** I have empowered you to think and act differently when making your daily personal finance decisions.

Unfortunately, many people equate money with power, but please keep in mind that having money doesn't guarantee eternal happiness.

In whatever you choose to do throughout your life, always be sure that it makes you happy—it is this feeling that will provide joy in your life and in the lives of those around you.

Last but certainly not least, be sure to share your time and talents with your family, friends, community, state, nation, and the world. Together we can empower others to make this world a better place in which to live.

Glossary of Terms

401(k): A retirement account offered by most publicly and privately owned organizations. Many times, participating organizations will match the amount of your pre-tax contribution (within specified limits).

403(b): A retirement account offered by most not-for-profit organizations. Many times, participating organizations will match the amount of your pre-tax contribution (within specified limits).

Adjustable Rate Mortgage: An interest rate on a loan that does not remain fixed but rather adjusts at pre-determined times to current market interest rates.

Appraisal: When purchasing a home and applying for a loan, the bank determines the value of the property by ordering a professional appraisal.

Annual Fee: A fee charged by a majority of credit card companies to use their cards. These fees can range anywhere from $10 to $150 (and higher!) annually depending on the type of credit card you use.

ATM (Automated Teller Machine) Card: This card can be used at ATMs to withdraw money, make deposits, and check your account balance.

Bounced Check: A check that is rejected and returned if sufficient funds are not available in the account from which it was written.

Certificate of Deposit: A savings account that offers competitive interest rates to customers based on the amount they deposit. Traditional CDs lock in your money for a predetermined amount of time and impose a penalty for early withdrawals; Liquids CDs allow more flexibility to withdraw funds without a fee but at a lower interest rate.

Charge Card: This card is commonly offered at department and specialty stores and requires that the balance due be paid off at the end of each month.

Check Register: A spreadsheet that allows you to list all of your deposits and withdrawals, including those from an ATM and debit card transactions, while keeping a running balance of funds that remain in your account.

Collections Agency: If a credit account balance is seriously overdue, this type of agency will attempt to collect the money owed, charge you a ton of fees, and take action to negatively impact your credit score.

Credit Card: A convenient payment method that charges a finance fee if the balance due is not paid in full at the end of each month.

Credit History Report: An outline of all your open, closed, and delinquent credit accounts (credit cards, auto loans, student loans, home loans). It includes a history of all of your accounts, how much you currently owe, how many times you have made late payments, and when they occurred.

Credit Score (also known as FICO Score): A score ranging from 300 to 850 based on the contents of your credit history report. The higher the score, the less risk you are to creditors, and the better the chance you have to borrow money at a lower interest rate.

Debit Card: This card can be used as an ATM card as well as a credit card wherever your card is accepted (Visa or MasterCard).

Direct Deposit: A paycheck that is electronically deposited into your bank account.

Dividends: Monetary earnings that a company distributes to its stockholders when they feel as though they will not be using those funds for investments in the near future.

Equity: The difference between the amount an investment is currently worth and what was originally paid for the investment.

Escrow Company: An independent party that acts as the intermediary for the transfer of funds between the bank, the buyer, and the seller for transactions involving the purchase and sale of a home.

FACT (Fair and Accurate Credit Transactions Act of 2003): Under this act, you are entitled to a free copy of your credit history report from each of the three major credit-reporting agencies (Equifax, Experian, and TransUnion) once a year.

FAFSA (Free Application for Federal Student Aid): The only way you will be considered for federal student loans is if you and your parent(s) fill out the FAFSA, which is full of all sorts of personal and financial questions to better assess your financial needs. The application becomes available on January 1 for use for the next academic year and can be found at: www.fafsa.ed.gov.

FDIC (Federal Deposit Insurance Corporation): This is a federal organization that insures your individual bank account balances up to $250,000.

Finance Fee: A pre-determined percentage fee imposed by credit card companies on the remaining balance if the total balance due is not paid in full at the end of each month.

Fixed Rate: An interest rate on a loan that remains constant throughout the duration of the loan.

Identification (ID) Theft: If your social security number, credit card, bank card, check book, bank statements, or any other item that may contain personal information gets in the hands of the wrong person, your identity and money can be compromised.

Installment Payment: An account, such as an auto or home loan, with a fixed payment amount for a pre-determined amount of time.

Late Fee: This is a fee for not making a credit card payment on time and can range anywhere from $15 to $45 (and higher!).

Lease: A contract under which one pays a mutually agreed upon amount of money to borrow a car, apartment, or house for a fixed amount of time.

Mutual Fund: A stock and/or government bond investment account that pools money together from thousands of people and is managed by a fund manager.

NSF (Non-Sufficient Funds) Fee: An account fee charged if one does not have the funds available in their account to pay a check presented for deposit or to be cashed. This fee applies to all future transactions so long as the account has a negative balance.

Overdrawn Account: When your account balance falls below $0.00, you will incur a fee of around $20-$30 (perhaps higher!) for each transaction that is paid and processed when you carry a negative balance.

Overdraft Protection: This protects you from expensive fees incurred when overdrawing your account by either transferring money from an existing savings account or charging the amount due to a credit card that you authorized to be opened at your bank.

Perkins Loan: A subsidized federal student loan that requires applicants to fill out the FAFSA and show financial need to pay for their education.

PIN (Personal Identification Number) Code: A secret access code encrypted into your ATM/debit card to provide extra security when you use your card at an ATM or to make purchases.

PLUS (Parent Loan for Undergraduate Students): An unsubsidized federal student loan that requires applicants to fill out the FAFSA and one's parent(s) to have a very good credit history.

Private Mortgage Insurance (PMI): Required by home loan companies when your down payment is less than 20% of the value of the home. This insures the value of the loan because the amount of money that is owed to lenders is very high.

Reason Codes: Each credit agency will provide you with a few reasons why your credit score is not higher than it could be. If your credit score is low, these codes are certainly helpful to getting you on the right path toward improving your credit score.

Returned Check Fee: The person that deposits a check that bounces will be charged this fee from their bank.

Revolving Payment: An account, such as a credit card, with a payment amount due that fluctuates according to monthly usage.

Roth IRA: An investment account that offers tax-free withdrawal of funds at or after age 59 ½ though annual account contributions are fully taxable.

Secured Credit Card: A method of establishing your credit history by securing your expenses with an amount you deposit in a linked account. Used just like a normal credit card, you will receive a monthly statement to pay off a portion or all of your debts.

Stafford Loan: A subsidized or unsubsidized federal student loan that requires applicants to fill out the FAFSA and show financial need to pay for their education.

Stop Payment: When you notify your bank to not cash a stolen or wrongfully written check.

Subsidized Loan: A feature on a student loan in which the government pays for all the interest incurred throughout your time in college.

Title Company: A company that guarantees that a property is successfully transferred into your name with ONLY the home loan(s) you applied for when purchasing a home.

Traditional IRA: An investment account that offers annual tax-deductible contributions though withdrawals after retirement are fully taxable.

Unsubsidized Loan: A feature on a student loan in which the person receiving the funds is responsible for paying all the interest incurred, though all payments can be deferred until after graduation.

REFERENCES

Stock Price: Fair Isaac Corporation (FICO). Retrieved May 25, 2011 from http://money.cnn.com/quote/quote. html?symb=FICO

Student Aid on the Web: Funding your Education. Retrieved February 11, 2011 from www.FederalStudentAid.ed.gov/ funding

Student Debt and the Class of 2009. Retrieved March 2, 2011 from http://projectonstudentdebt.org/files/pub/classof2009.pdf

Study finds rising number of college students using credit cards for tuition. Retrieved March 2, 2011 from https://www1. salliemae.com/about/news_info/newsreleases/041309.htm

What's in your credit report. Retrieved January 3, 2011 from http://www.myfico.com/CreditEducation/InYourReport. aspx

What's in your FICO score. Retrieved January 3, 2011 from http:// www.myfico.com/CreditEducation/WhatsInYourScore.aspx

Your Insured Deposits: Ownership Categories. Revocable Trust Accounts. Retrieved January 2, 2011 http://www.fdic.gov/ deposit/deposits/insured/ownership4.html

Disclaimer

The accuracy and completeness of the information provided herein and opinions stated herein are not guaranteed or warranted to produce any particular results. The advice and strategies contained herein may not be suitable for every individual. The author shall not be liable for any loss incurred as a consequence of the use and application, directly or indirectly, of any information presented in this work. Generally, this book is sold with the understanding that the author is not engaged in rendering legal, accounting, financial planning, or any kind of professional services.

In addition, this book does not make any recommendation or endorsement as to any investment, advisor, or other service or product. In addition, this book does not offer any advice regarding the nature, potential value, or suitability of any particular investment, security, or investment strategy, all of which should be specifically addressed to the reader's own financial advisor.

Photo Credit

Front and Back Cover Photos by:

Angus Ross Photography

Special Thanks

Christopher Hale

CPSIA information can be obtained at www.ICGtesting.com
Printed in the USA
269629BV00001B/16/P